Ten Years Later

Personal Lessons from a Decade of Life, Research and Ministry

by George Barna

GEORGE BARNA

Ten Years Later

Personal Lessons from a Decade of Life, Research and Ministry

aBarnaReport

Published by Barna Research Group, Ltd.
647 West Broadway • Glendale, CA 91204-1007

Printed in the United States. ISBN 1-882297-01-6

ISBN 1-882297-01-6

Acknowledgments

This book is, for me, a bit quirky. And without the help of a few special people, it would have been much quirkier.

Gwen Ingram challenged a lot of the content in the earlier manuscript, encouraging me to be more clear and more rational. And if I had taken her advice more often, she probably would have succeeded. Thanks, Gwen.

Paul Rottler put some visual zip into a flat document. Did it just about overnight, too. Colorado's nice, Paul, but it's too small to contain a man of your enormous talent. Stay in here in Los Angeles.

Ron Sellers used *Strunk and White* and a red pen to assail my grammar and punctuation (or lack of them). Really, I *do* know the language, Ron. I'm just trying to keep you busy.

Nancy Barna gave her usual honest feedback on some of the lessons found herein...and I'm still smarting from the *new* lessons she taught me (in humility, style, etc.).

What a great partner in life! Thanks, Nancy, for doing everything you can to support what I'm trying to do. You've earned a vacation. (What, you want me to *accompany* you on it? But I've got three more book deadlines this month and an elders meeting and...)

The rest of the gang at Barna Research is pretty darn outrageous, too. Problem is, I don't hang out there enough these days to know who they are or what they really do... Well, that's *their* version. Thanks, Vibeke Klocke, Cindy Coats, Keith Deaville, George Maupin, Telford Work, and Vince Vaughan. Without you and your predecessors, I never would have had the opportunity to learn half of these lessons.

May whatever I have learned in the past ten years make my time with each of you more rewarding in the coming ten.

Contents

Preface
13

Lessons about Life
19

People
65

Leadership
81

Religion and Church Life
121

Conclusion
149

Preface

A few months ago I heard a presentation delivered by a veteran pastor. He was leading a training session for other pastors, and was describing a particularly difficult period in his own life during which he seriously questioned his call to full-time ministry. Part of his response to the situation was to set aside a few hours to ponder the various things he had learned in his years of ministry. He described his reflections and noted that he was so encouraged by all he had learned that he decided it was worth staying the course.

Frankly, I wondered about his decision. It seemed to me that if he was so shaken by his sense of inefficacy that he had to make a conscious effort to identify any lessons he had learned, well, perhaps he had forgotten more than he had actually "learned."

Nevertheless, his inspired approach sounded like a great concept: taking time to reflect over many years of highs and lows to intentionally identify the seeds of wisdom and insight borne from those experiences. It struck me as a wonderful idea because it seems that most of us live life on the run, struggling to make it from one moment to the next without some major catastrophe or crisis getting the best of us. We rarely have (or, at least, take) the time to put our engines in neutral long enough to get a good assessment of where we have been, and what that should have taught us about where we're going and how we'll get there.

With this concept in mind, I sat down and over the course of a few days (it seems I've forgotten more than the pastor whose idea I was mimicking!) tried to identify some notions or principles that had been ingrained in my mind over the last decade. That ten-year block of time represents the period since departing graduate school and entering the real world: working full-time, striving to discover, to achieve and to grow. Without summarily demeaning the value of some of my previous writing, my desire was to get beyond the ideas I had addressed in past books and identify other lessons that I might more typically overlook or downplay.

The relative brevity of this book is probably the single most profound statement about my ability to absorb new lessons from a decade of experiences and adventures! However, not a writer who enjoys "fluffing up" the text, my decision was to leave the text on the thin side rather than artificially create new "insights" or rattle on with compelling but imaginary anecdotes that prove the point.

Let's be honest: this is neither heady nor profound stuff. It is one man's simple reflections on what he has enjoyed and endured over a ten-year period. Hopefully, though, some of these recollections or perspectives may ignite a mental chain reaction for you that will remind you of, or facilitate the clarification of, some lessons that you have mastered in your own travails.

Why bother? Because increasingly, I am persuaded that we repeat the same mistakes more than we realize. (Sadly, this seems even more true within the Church than outside of it.) The mechanism that enables such repetition is our failure to recall what we have encountered or to own the lessons of our personal past. Maybe by witnessing just how unprofound or unsophisticated my lessons are, you will be encouraged to reflect on your life's journey. (In other words, taking the "hey, I can do better than that" approach.) Indeed, in the course of doing this, I have already noticed the benefit of re-living, albeit painfully in a few cases, both the good and bad of my days past, toward revising my course of action for the days future.

By the way, some of what you read in these pages is decidedly tongue-in-cheek. In the interests of having a good time (although, perhaps, a dangerous one for my reputation), I'll let you decide which of the thoughts contained within this volume are serious and which are of a lighter vein.

The lessons are divided into four broad areas: those related to life, in general; to people; to leadership; and to religion and the Church.

May you be challenged into a fuller examination of who you are, how you live, and what you might do to make the most of your remaining time.

Lessons
About
Life

Lesson

The most effective things in life are usually simple.

Over the last several years, many church leaders and consultants have visited with me to discuss their latest ideas regarding new methods for ministry impact. More often than not, I emerge with a pounding headache. I'm basically a simple person. Even if I have the capacity to perform the mental gymnastics required to comprehend the latest and greatest strategies for church growth, capital funds campaigns, assimilation, and the like, I hate to expend the effort. When I am conned into trying, I find that usually it is not worth the effort.

It has taken me a decade or so to realize that the best plans are the simplest, and the most effective strategies are based primarily upon common sense. It's not that there is anything wrong or inherently evil about complicated strategies. It's just that they usually don't work. They offer too many opportunities for things to break down or fall apart.

Or, the solution—being more complex than the problem in many cases—simply does not have all the loose ends tied together.

Life is too fast, too complex and requires too much input from the most fallible of entities (human beings) to allow for most complex approaches to make a big impact.

To many people (especially the typical consultant), this is pure heresy. "Barna has gone soft," I can hear them crying. Truth be known, I would have sided with them just a few years back, verbally lashing out at the simpletons who rallied behind the most simple (not to be confused with simplistic) solutions possible.

Years of graduate school had pushed me to think in terms of the multi-layered models of reality. Those who couldn't comprehend these painstakingly developed constructs were probably intellectually inferior. We would have to do the job in spite of them, rather than through them, I reasoned. But such, I continued in my arrogance, was the beauty of being a leader. We understood the problems, we called the shots, we took the responsibility, we received the joy of success.

By now I have been out of the academic haven long enough to have been first perplexed, then devastated, by the consistent failure of such complex-is-better thinking. And I have worked with a sufficient number of skilled, intelligent leaders who repeatedly achieve success through the application of simple truths and solutions to recognize the ignorance of my past.

Fortunately, God broke through with this concept early in my life. I would not be a Christian today if it were not for my acceptance of the value of simplicity. At the time that I accepted Christ as my Savior, I was in grad school. Through a series of circumstances, I left the church in which I had been raised and went on a religious pilgrimage, not even sure what I was searching for. Eventually, I wound up at a Bible-teaching church that kept harping on the importance of Jesus and eternal salvation.

One night, the pastor and elders visited with my wife and me to answer our questions about these matters. They spent an hour earnestly discussing creation, life's purpose, the role of the Bible, Jesus' life and death and resurrection, and the decision that I had to make about who He was and what my life was about. At first, I was totally stumped by this incredible no-risk offer: eternal salvation, mine free for the asking. After some hesitation, I agreed to admit that I was a sinner and needed forgiveness (that was the easy part), and that I would commit my life to following Jesus and accepted a life with Him in heaven as part of the deal.

Believe it or not, I told the elders and pastor that it seemed like a set up, too good to be true. "Men," I skeptically and pompously explained, "what you're proposing is just too simple. I spend my life studying people's behavior and their decisions and their mistakes. The great things in life are never this easy. And this proposition you're offering seems ridiculously easy."

Realize, I'm a 24-year old kid sitting there at the kitchen table with these relative strangers who are each old enough to be my father. I'm thinking about all the stuff that has gone down in my life, wondering if it were possible to wipe the slate clean, like they were claiming. The intellectual jousting was a front for my abject fear that these individuals were suggesting that a deep, long-term problem (my apparent separation from God) might have an immediate, permanent solution that was unbelievably simple.

The time had come for a decision. "I don't know if what you're saying is true. But I'll give God 30 days to prove Himself to be who and what you say He is. This is either the most absurd and naive claim of the century, or a once-in-a-lifetime deal. I figure I've got nothing to lose here. Count me in."

Well, these men of God were not ecstatic about my approach, but they encouraged me to take this leap of faith and to commit myself totally to the new life I was praying God to deliver. It was the simplest of offers in response to a complex history of sin, rebellion, and rejection. But it was my first inkling of how a simple answer to a complex problem may be the most effective way of handling a thorny situation.

Simple does not mean simplistic. Simple may still be sophisticated, but it carefully avoids convolution.

My recent studies of effective leadership have led me to conclude that one mark of a truly brilliant strategist or leader is the ability to analyze a complex problem and develop a creative but simple solution. That research has also shown that brilliant leaders often go unnoticed because their solutions appear deceptively simple. The truth is that simple solutions are hard work. But they are worth the effort.

My advice to those who make decisions is to examine all the options and arrive at a conclusion which makes the complex as simple as possible. Why? Because simplicity works.

Lesson

Patience is sometimes over-rated.

I don't have the patience for patience.

I recognize that patience is a good character trait. And I will readily acknowledge that exhibiting patience can have some mighty positive effects in many situations. In fact, I am awfully appreciative that God, Himself, demonstrated long-term patience with me, waiting for me to come to the realization that He is God and I am not. Seems I was confused about that for a long time...

Consider the difficulties caused by the exercise of patience.

- A leader must wait for all of the sluggards to catch up, to see what he or she noticed long ago, before real progress can be made.

- A consultant must wait for the client to grasp the application of a process, or the implications of key information, or the significance of outcomes.

- A pastor must suffer interminable committee meetings, most of which should never have been scheduled in the first place.

- A counselor must endure the senseless repetition of tangential stories, over and over again.

- A consumer must wait for a salesperson with the IQ of a fried vegetable to get the order right.

The hard truth is that some leaders may well lose their edge toward creating change, lasting impact and widespread satisfaction when they substitute patience for honesty and timely perseverance. There is the balance to be achieved between sensitivity and productivity, certainly; there is no virtue in stomping on other people in the mad rush to achieve one's goals quickly.

However, to our detriment, I think we often go soft on achievement and personal growth, leaning instead toward the assumption that irritation with poor performance, failure to learn from mistakes, and a hard-nosed commitment to otherwise laudable objectives reflects an "ungodly character."

Frankly, I fail to see Jesus' patience with the Pharisees and Sadducees, or His patience with Peter's ignorance. I have trouble finding Paul's patience with Peter's prejudices. (Peter seemed to bring out the impatience in people.) Yes, I realize that patience is listed among the "fruits of the Spirit," but also cannot help but think that there are times when too much patience stands in the way of bearing the other fruits.

Anyway, without resorting to proof-texting, it seems reasonable to expect us to strive to learn how and when to use patience, but to limit its application to those times when it is truly appropriate, not simply when it is socially acceptable or publicly noticed. Maybe what I'm searching for is a model of "loving impatience": an ability to know when patience will result in a distortion of truth and reality, and when it represents the more defensible path to a desirable outcome. We'd all be better off if sometimes we were not the recipients of undeserved patience, but instead were lovingly (if impatiently) held accountable for our behavior by someone who justifiably loses his or her patience over unnecessary or unreasonable behavior.

Lesson

If everybody loves you, you're probably not doing anything worthwhile.

In studying effective leaders, one of the things I've discovered is that they are willing to be misunderstood and disliked by others as a result of their unshakable conviction in what they are doing.

I've also found that when people are receiving virtually unlimited praise from the masses, one of two things has happened: they have developed the cure for cancer (or something of a similar magnitude), or they are a "yes" person, striving to please people, but accomplishing little of value in the process.

Granted, sometimes you will experience a mix of praise and derision. This, in fact, may be the best indication that you are not simply regurgitating what others have already laid out, but are doing so in a more effective manner or are actually pushing the boundaries a bit.

How sad it is when I encounter someone who gauges his or her impact on the basis of whether or not people love them or accept their aggregate effort. In almost every such case I have explored, the individual has virtually ceased to have any true direction, vision, or desire to challenge others. Instead, their purpose is to gain the comfortable applause of individuals who are neither threatened nor stimulated by the work of the "leader."

Naturally, this can be taken too far. Sometimes I encounter those irascible, contentious individuals whose sole purpose in life, it seems, is to aggravate everyone else. That, to me, is no virtue, either. As they spend their time attempting to undermine the well-intentioned efforts and work of others, or to steal every potential morsel of joy and satisfaction from life, they lose sight of the bigger purpose of life.

Having said this, I suppose the natural conclusion is that there is virtue in balance. Few things in life are exclusively positive or negative. While such one-sided characterizations may sometimes bring notoriety or attention to an individual, such a portrayal ultimately becomes a caricature. Caricatures are, of course, fun to play with and easy to remember. But who among us wants to actually become such a uni-dimensional, unfulfilled person?

The bottom line, then, must be that we deal honestly with our reality—call good things "good" and bad things "bad." But strive for a balance in perspective that enables us to absorb all that God has intended for us. And that includes taking some heat for an unpopular view that reflects our integrity.

Lesson

If you don't believe in yourself, you cannot expect others to believe in you, either.

Of the Ten Commandments for True Fulfillment, the most important of these is to believe in God with all your heart, soul and mind. And the second is like it: believe in yourself.

What frequently differentiates winners and losers is their tenacity. That ability to pursue a goal or a dream unwaveringly is closely related to how deeply the individual believes in himself or herself. The achievers of the world, and those who really seem to squeeze the greatest joy and fulfillment from their days on this planet, are those who recognize that they are not perfect but they are valuable and capable.

Some of the most pathetic memories I have are of interacting with individuals, mostly political candidates, low-level corporate managers, and pastors, who have no self-confidence. The catch-22 of their circumstance is that they are waiting for others to believe in them, so that they can be convinced to believe in themselves. In my observation, the chances are pretty overwhelming that it just ain't gonna happen.

Many people I've worked with have taken to describing me as an entrepreneur. That may be. But I was not always that way. I come from a family in which *risk* is a four-letter word. And although my family was very supportive of me and did a wonderful job of facilitating a strong, positive self-image, my early inclinations were to seek the safe route in the working world.

But after watching the behavior and the outcomes related to those who believed in themselves and those who did not, it became apparent to me. One of the keys to making it in this world is to accept who you are—warts, pimples, flab, and all the rest—and determine how you can convert your positive attributes into success. I was greatly encouraged in this by discovering successful individuals who had less going for them than I thought I had in my asset ledger. Obviously, if they could do it, I could.

Believing in myself has enabled me to ignore the naysayers who argued that because I was only 21 years old I couldn't successfully manage election campaigns. That I couldn't complete two graduate degrees simultaneously. That I could not start and lead a successful research company in Los Angeles. That nobody would be willing to read my books because they were tainted by research statistics and charts. That I could never afford to buy a house in the inflated Los Angeles real estate market. And so forth. Little obstacles, each of these, but compacted together they could have been the mountain that collapsed on all of my hopes for the kind of life I wanted to live.

Naturally, my faith in Christ has been the crucial part of the story. What a mind-blower to discover that not only did the God of the universe create me, but *He* believed in me enough to send Christ to die for me, *personally*, and to give me the freedom to be whatever got my juices running. It's awfully easy to give up on yourself these days, unless you know that in the eyes of the Savior of the world, you're precious and important.

At some point, I think you need to adopt a hybrid philosophy that blends the eternal and the mundane. For me, it went like this: since God Himself loves me, I must be a person of worth. And since He has given me His stamp of approval, freedom to act, and natural talents, I'd better not squander the opportunities I have. It's important to pick myself up by my bootstraps and get on with life.

To me, believing in yourself is kind of a modern-day Pascal's Wager. If you whole-heartedly believe in yourself, and make a play for the things in life that are meaningful to you, you might achieve it all, so you win. If you whole-heartedly believe in yourself, and go for the gold, you might not achieve your goals, but you're likely to be better off than if you never made the attempt. But if you whole-heartedly doubt yourself, even your best effort will be half-baked, so you're quite likely to lose.

Americans have fine-tuned the art of sensing when another person views himself as a loser. And we have elevated to the status of science the ability to support that negative self-view.

It seems only sensible to do whatever you can to believe in yourself. No one else will until you take that risk.

Lesson

It's important to have fun on the job; it prevents burnout and ruptured relationships— both of which are likely as the pressure mounts.

I have had the opportunity to work within several large organizations, and to spend many days inside other global organizations, observing first-hand what it's like to work there. My conclusion?

I own a small company. And it is small by choice.

Only on rare occasions do I find a large organization that, as part of its corporate culture, has determined that its employees must have fun on the job. But what could be more likely to motivate good work and a sense of corporate loyalty than allowing people to do what they do best, and to do it in an environment which endorses fun?

From my own experience, I've learned that small does not have to mean "limited." On a per-employee basis, we're probably about as productive as they come. Part of that output is a direct result of the fact that we have tried so hard to spread both responsibility and authority, and to balance it with a sense of enjoyment over what we do.

I guess that means enjoying each other, enjoying the nature of the work, enjoying the sense of impact that our work creates, enjoying relationships with our clients, and enjoying the ability of God to use each of us in a special way toward achieving corporate ends that far exceed what any of us might achieve separately.

One of the greatest benefits of permitting—nay, pursuing—fun at the place of work is the stability of the workplace relationships. When the pressure mounts—and it seems inevitably to do so—the potential for broken relationships within the team soars. Why? Because the emotional distance between employees was never bridged, resulting in an inability to gain fulfillment from our internal relationships.

When the tough times surround us, we have emerged as superior to the challenge largely because of the relationships built among the staff. And a large part of that capacity is related to laboring in an environment where excellence is expected, but enjoyment is demanded. Work is important, but it is not the paramount consideration in life. Work, as a penalty to mankind, becomes less burdensome when it is put in perspective.

Do your best, and enjoy the process.

Lesson

Experts usually aren't.

Have you ever noticed that when a person writes a book, they're suddenly deemed an expert in their field? Or when the media interview someone for their opinion on an issue, their esteem in the eyes of their colleagues and among the population at large rises a level or two?

No one is more sensitive to this absurdity than I. Ten years ago, I was a skinny, bespectacled kid with a few degrees who was trying to sneak into concerts at Central Park. Today, I'm a skinny, bespectacled husband and father, wearing a shirt with a collar and (when forced to) a tie. Oh, yes, and I've written a few books. Whammo! Suddenly, people who wouldn't send me a job application five years ago are hailing me as an insightful leader in the evangelical community. Why? Because I had the temerity to hire a staff to dial telephones to ask thousands of randomly selected people from across the nation what they think on a range of issues, spent a little time thinking about their answers, spent a lot more time trying to write coherently about it, and was lucky enough to get a few publishers to chop down a forest or two to get those words out.

It's not just me, either. Look at some of the other "experts" we have today. Marketers shamelessly peddling their wares in print, when the media suddenly confuse them for professionals. Clergy who preach a few good sermons, then have their staff transcribe the tapes and edit it all together as a book. Former mid-level managers who leave (or are asked to leave) their jobs at large organizations and, in a last ditch effort to capture attention for their fledgling "consulting" firms, get an article or book published which then pushes them down the path of experthood. Professors who read enough papers on a given topic by their students that they magically erupt with an idea that becomes a book, a public presentation or some other media-exalted conceptualization.

I began to notice in the seventies that we ceased to talk about stars and instead looked for superstars. We rejected the large church and went in search of the mega-church. Bingo was replaced by the million-dollar lotteries. I think it was around that time that we also eased the qualifications for an expert. I missed the ad, but it must have read something like this:

"Expert wanted: must be breathing; speak in full or partial sentences; pepper the language with industry jargon; tell colorful, if irrelevant stories; personally know an industry giant; desire to spend gobs of time in media interviews."

Watch out for the experts. I think we're living in the era of the professional expert, the individual who has no real craft but can tell you everything you want to know about someone else's. And don't worry, if you can't get the insight you need from an expert, just hire a consultant...

Lesson

Pick your fights.

By nature, I'm contentious. *You have a problem with that?*

Part of my dilemma is that I take things very literally. The other part is that I tend to be somewhat of a perfectionist. Put these two extremes together and you have one long night anytime you hope to engage me in a breezy, free-wheeling and pleasurable conversation.

It has been tough for me to recognize that these tendencies can really hold me back in life. I get so caught up in the minutia of the moment that I lose the big picture. Or, I see the fault in a peripheral aspect of your argument and assume that your entire polemic is worthless.

Actually, it was while I was working with a person at Disney who had some of these same character traits that I realized I'd better come up with a strategy to compensate for my own frailties, or I'd wind up in a fight to the finish with this, my biggest client. After toying with the adversary a bit, I finally came to a simple but invaluable realization.

To succeed in life, you have to pick your fights. Carefully.

"Carefully," not because you want to back down from those who will push you to your limit or possibly even defeat you. "Carefully" because many of the fights or disagreements in which you can become embroiled over the course of an average day are simply not worth the effort.

It's like my dog, Maxwell. A pleasant enough fellow, Max is. A bit shy on the cerebral side, though. He will spend four, sometimes five hours chasing down a lizard in our backyard. The spirit of the hunt, I suppose. But since the objective is to feed on the lizard, if we do a cost-benefit analysis of the transaction, Max probably expends about 20 units of energy in return for the two units of energy that eating the lizard will replenish. Not a very good exchange. Luckily for Max, I feed him every night regardless of his daily lizard count.

The principle of picking your fights has paid off mightily for me over the past couple of years. To the untrained eye, this philosophy appears to have actually softened me a bit. The truth is that by sizing up the ultimate value of a potential victory in cost-benefit terms, I avoid many unnecessary confrontations.

By the way, I have discovered that there is an excellent alternative to using the "pick your fights" strategy.

Own the company. It's amazing how often that mere fact will eliminate unwarranted discussions.

Lesson

It's true; you really can't believe everything you read.

One of my wife's elderly relatives once made a fascinating statement: "It wouldn't be in the newspaper if it wasn't true." What made the statement all the more intriguing was that her "newspaper" was one of the supermarket tabloids that was proclaiming the recent landing of three-headed aliens from a distant planet.

This woman may have been a bit naive, but she was no idiot. In fact, I respected her wisdom in many dimensions of life. (Not her choice of reading materials or her definition of reliable sources of scientific reality, perhaps, but of other aspects of life.)

Having spent a decade exploring the guts of a variety of major organizations—in my case, political campaigns, media outlets, advertising agencies, Christian ministries, non-profit organizations, and major manufacturers—you quickly shed that childlike confidence in others and start trying to peer through the darkness to see just what evil lurks beyond the shadows.

Lately, I've been struck by the pervasiveness of lies. And I've also been struck by how often I still get sucked in by a good fable. Here are just a few myths that I have recently had to unmask for myself.

Myth #1

When an esteemed Christian ministry or non-profit organization sends me an "audited" financial statement, the figures on the page are believable.

Unfortunately, some organizations dissect their fundraising costs and lump a substantial proportion of those costs under an innocuous category known as "public education." In that way, they can maintain the claim that they spend "less than 20% of all donated funds" on fundraising. Through creative accounting, donors will never know just how little of their money actually gets used for ministry.

Myth #2

Authors write their own books.

You might be amazed at how many books are ghost-written. It's just as common among Christian authors as it is among academicians and other authors. Few people—and I mean very few—have ever accused me of being traditional in my thinking, but I do confess to a weakness for wanting the author to write his or her own book. It's that integrity thing. Just doesn't seem very ethical for a person who did not write the book to have their name plastered all over the front cover. Even when they claim that the ideas expressed in the book were originally thoughts that they outlined for the real writer of the volume.

(By the way, let me answer that question going through your mind at this moment. I have written every word of every book that has come out with my name on it. Really, I have.)

Myth #3

When ministries raise money for a project, all the money raised goes to that project.

Sadly, there are a few ministries I know which use particular forms of ministry simply because those types of programs or projects are effective for fundraising. They have little regard for the quality or scope of the ministry being conducted.

Honestly, I really dislike having to be skeptical of everyone and everything. Unfortunately, the extensive degree of fraud and deception in our society almost demands any thinking individual to assume such defensiveness. This cynicism and disbelief among people is one of the root causes of the sense of alienation among Americans.

So how can we best handle the competing desires for self-protection through skepticism and cultural bonding through trust?

Perhaps we have to be more committed to digging for information beneath the surface level before making a decision. And we might best accomplish this by assuming that the better informed we are, the better decisions we will make.

And maybe we can mutually agree that the buck stops with us, so we will not engage in any form of deception in our own dealings with people and institutions. After all, the best form of education is modeling. If we model vulnerability and integrity in every transaction in our daily activities, maybe it will catch on. At the very least, we will have played a role in furthering honesty through example, rather than deceit by default.

Lesson

Every trial brings with it a lesson. Learn the lesson quickly and so minimize your chances of having to re-live the trial on another day.

Like most people, I am not especially fond of suffering and personal trials. If there is an escape clause, I'll probably find it. You've heard about the guy who always takes the easy route. I designed the map.

Until, that is, I noticed a pattern in my life. Thank God I'm analytical to a fault or I'd still be plagued with this condition. The pattern was that I'd encounter a trial, endure some suffering, moan and groan about it, and try to distance myself as far and as quickly from the situation as possible. Never a trace of interest in discovering the bottom-line lesson involved. Much more interest in discovering the border line of the nearest comfort zone.

Then, flash, the light bulb above the head went on and it all became clear to me. (All right, we'll give scripture some credit for this one, too.) God uses pain, suffering, trials and failures as a way of maturing us. Eww, did I hate the thought. But it's true.

So, being the analytical, Type A personality that I am, I decided that a new philosophy of life was called for. I even shared it with the staff one day, I was so attached to this discovery. "When you hit the wall," I boldly told them, "learn the lesson God wants to teach you and move on. Maybe that way, you won't have to go through that experience again."

As is their habit, they stared at me and politely nodded their assent. They're used to this sort of brilliance-of-the-moment proclamation from me. They humor me. I love them.

Lesson

The best reason to study history may simply be to grasp the big picture. Only then can you understand just how insignificant, in the long-run, today's crises really are.

It is simply too easy to get caught up in the emotion of the moment.

They say we're living in the Information Age. I don't doubt it for a moment. With all the publications, the new electronic media, the vast array of surveys and other data-producing entities, the computer technologies for slicing and dicing information—there's more than anyone can handle.

But the most important consequence of the avalanche of information, I think, is the fact that now we have to make decisions much more quickly and efficiently than ever. In the past, we could bluff our way through the process for a few days while waiting for the pertinent information to arrive. Then we could wheeze our way through another day or two of discussions before arriving at a final determination. Time may have been of the essence, but we seemed to have more essence in the past.

Now, we have no time to gather or interpret. If we wait too long, a competitor will act more swiftly, positioning us as an outsider or an also-ran. Too little, too late.

So, to me, the benefit of history is to place all of this in context. Sometimes I find myself getting bent out of shape because my staff or I did not respond quickly enough to what might have been a sterling opportunity. At the time, I can see nothing other than the flashing neon sign before my eyes that reads,

MISSED OPPORTUNITY. LOSER. LOSER. LOSER.

By God's grace, though, my company has survived the truckload of missed opportunities over the past couple of years and has actually thrived. Perhaps it's His way of telling me that when I grasp the big picture, as in His view of what matters and how things really work, those glitches were insignificant.

In those oh-so-rare moments when I stop temporarily and push my ego out of the way long enough to strive to see things from God's perspective, I recognize that there are relatively few matters of earth-shattering importance. Further, I admit that many more events than you might imagine are fairly predictable, based on what we know of

God, His plans for mankind, mankind's typical responses to God, and the law of averages.

In the end, I want my life to count for something bigger than a tombstone that proclaims,

GEORGE BARNA LIVED AND DIED.
HERE ARE HIS NUMBERS...

If I can just remain centered on God's vision for my life and ministry, and keep trying to chip away at all the truth He has for me to ingest through His Word, and live with commitment and passion, it'll all work out.

But, man, is it hard sometimes to overlook those blown chances. If I didn't know better, I'd think I really could have changed the world by mastering that opportunity.

Lesson

Anyone who accomplishes more than average must not have children living in their home.

For the first thirteen years of my marriage, everything was copacetic. A great wife who was immersed in the business with me. An unusually high degree of productivity at work. A loving God, good friends, supportive extended family, comfortable home, two wonderful dogs, decent income, good health, and two excellent guitars.

And then it happened. Our first child arrived.

Don't misunderstand me. I love our daughter. She is cute, lovable, fun, challenging, an answer to prayer. I would not trade her in, even for a third excellent guitar.

But I can trace my decline in productivity to the day she arrived. She may be cute and lovable, but she's also treading on Daddy-the-Achiever's sacred turf.

Someday I hope to gain a grant from an overfunded foundation to study the effects of the first-born on every Daddy's ability to maintain the same levels of concentration, energy, and output as before the arrival of the child. And before conducting the study I hope to find a bookie in Vegas who will give me good odds that fathers are more productive after the birth than before. You see, I've always wanted to retire early and this could be my ticket.

Anyway, if you have been struggling to reach your former levels of productivity at your work—whether you are responsible for creating scintillating sermons, selling widgets, or handling customers at the check-out line of the supermarket—I'm willing to bet that the cause of your demise is a recent addition to the family.

Among the sleep deprivation, financial jeopardy, language regression, and diaper dependency caused by the tot, the chances of maintaining your productivity are slim to none. When the first child arrives, you'd better have a great "plan B" in mind for how you expect to finish whatever you had started, and how you expect to accomplish whatever you had set your heart upon.

Hey, the apostle Paul knew what he was saying when he suggested that it is better to remain single, if possible, than to get married. In fact, that admonition may well be the best evidence in the Bible that he was actually a married man with kiddies crawling around his home...

Lesson

True innovators are a rare breed; clever impersonators of innovators are a dime a dozen.

I can probably count on two hands the number of people who, in the disciplines that I know the best, were true innovators.

When I was in grad school, I was tremendously impressed by people with degrees, by individuals who held lofty titles, and by contemporaries who had mastered the fast track to ascend to the top of their field in record time. Being young and impressionable, I hoped that someday I, too, might be able to live in the stratosphere of my industry's legends.

But as I became more immersed in my studies and eventually left the cozy cocoon of academia, I discovered that most of the "legends" were merely replicas of the real thing, simply pale shadows of the authentic movers and shakers of the world. The pretenders were simply place-holders. They filled a role, pompously in many cases, but were not really transforming the world around them.

The stand-ins were able to get away with their impersonation of brilliance because we live in a world starved for truly unique thought and action. Even those who provide a good facade can get more than their fair share of attention and appreciation. Yet, most of what passes for seminal scholarship and cutting edge creative thinking is nothing more than good incrementalism. Rather than generating entirely new and original forms of thought, product or action, these individuals offer a marginal improvement of, or cosmetic tinkering with, what a prior giant has previously created.

As my sojourn through the political, business, sociological and religious worlds continued, I became increasingly convinced that most of the people who had made a name for themselves were actually minor leaguers. Their contributions to their respective fields were worthy, mind you, but they were not breakthrough artists. In each of the fields I studied, there were just a very few who were so creative and so groundbreaking that they truly shaped the field.

I have been alternately overwhelmed, puzzled, surprised, angered, challenged, exhilarated, and educated by the work of people such as Amitai Etzioni, Robert Moses, George Gilder, David Ogilvy, and Dan Yankelovich. They are not household names, but their sharp insights have been digested, dissected and eventually regurgitated by other, better-known individuals to help change your world and mine.

The minor leaguers hogged the media attention and worked hard to get the professional awards and attention. They did so by taking the work of the innovators and rearranging a few ideas or applications to make it appear as if they were creating new frontiers. In some cases, I believe they really thought they had done something striking and original. In reality, they had simply lurched forward on the foundations provided by the authentic gains attributable to the innovators.

The true innovative thinkers and leaders are the ones whose work I have come to appreciate the most. They understand the game of life sufficiently to know that when you buy into the prevailing system, you ultimately sell out to it. That system can become irresistibly seductive. Few have the personal power to reject the lures—fame, fortune, comfort, prestige, opportunities—that accompany such adulation and acceptance. But true innovators are generally unaware of such peripheral factors because they respond to different motives and generally exist in a whole different plane of life. They are moved by the ability to restructure the playing field itself.

You see, the minor leaguers are thrilled to hear the crowd roaring its approval for their simply being on the field and playing the game. The major league innovators, though, don't even realize there is a crowd present. They're too busy creating a new stadium, a new ball field, a new game to play. The minor leaguer would change a small portion of the way the existing game is played. The true innovator would create an entirely new game.

So I ask myself, where are the innovators and true leaders in the Christian Church in America these days? Must we constantly amuse ourselves by simply trying to reshape the same old blob of playdough? Surely there is an innovator in our midst who can create a new substance for us to work with, or mold it in an entirely new shape.

I doubt that I have that innovative gift. I'm more of an incrementalist—not by desire, but by design. It saddens me, but I'll just have to make the most of it. I may be wacky, but I just don't seem to have that off-center, creative spark. But I think maybe I can do some good by recognizing the real innovators and leaders and supporting their efforts.

How will you respond to the incrementalists and the innovators? Have you figured out who they are and how they influence your thinking and your efforts? Perhaps the Church would be better off if us incrementalists let the innovators do their thing, and we exerted more of our energy to exposing and utilizing their products.

Lesson

There are two ways to get ahead in life: *work* hard or *schmooze* hard.

Forgive me for a page or so as I indulge in a bit of Baby Boomer whining.

When God created man, He did not create them equal. First, He created the achiever. The achiever was endowed with brains and reason. This being was capable of logical thought, focused attention, creative problem-solving, and the ability to set and meet realistic deadlines. The achiever was a hard worker and was committed to being a productive worker. God witnessed this creature, and it pleased Him.

But, being a God who enjoys life, He decided to make for the achiever a nemesis. And so He did. He created the schmoozer. The schmoozer was a fast-talker and quick thinker, but a lazy individual. The schmoozer was most adept at building relationships by buying lunches, dinners, drinks, trinkets, flowers, and anything else imaginable to persuade the potential mark that the schmoozer was really caring, competent and reliable.

Just to make things interesting, God allowed the schmoozer to reap rewards for his efforts. And to this day, the schmoozer fulfills his role as the nemesis of the hard worker. May the Day of Judgment come soon.

I don't know how many business lunches I've had over the last decade, but I do know that little perturbs me more than watching a master schmoozer playing the field. Because clients love to have their egos massaged and their tummies filled, the schmoozer often takes away potential clients from me, the hard worker. That outcome is like scraping fingernails down a chalkboard. I have no qualms whatsoever about losing a potential job to a qualified, heady competitor. But when a job slips away because I have been out-schmoozed (which, granted, is not tough), that gets me upset.

Fortunately, I have studied enough organizations to have learned that most of them do not grow because they keep repeating the same mistakes. Frankly, if I don't learn how to schmooze better, I'll be guilty of the same repetitive failure syndrome. My resolve: I must schmooze.

But the stark reality is that there is nothing more pathetic than a hard-core producer trying to switch roles and play the part of the schmoozer. It's like Fred Sanford trying to be a college president; Roseanne Barr studying for the bar exam (not *that* bar, I mean the legal profession's qualifying test); or Gilligan running for president. Not a pretty picture.

So, as Francis Schaeffer would ask, "how, then, shall we live?"

I have an idea.

I strongly suspect that most of the people reading this book are hard workers. (Schmoozers, after all, are not much when it comes to reading.) Here's the plan. We all agree to reject the sales pitches of the schmoozers. Oh, sure, let them ply us with great food and wonderful presents. Let them send a parlay of endearing words our way. But when the time comes to buy their products or close the deal, slam the door in their face. Refuse to do business with the schmoozers. Their products are usually inferior and they rarely meet the standards to which they had agreed.

The beauty of this plan is that in order to remain afloat, schmoozers will have to do business with their most difficult prey: other schmoozers.

Hold off on that Day of Judgment, after all...

Lesson

New York and Los Angeles are worlds apart.

I grew up in the northeast. Once I had completed my education, my wife and I packed up a rental truck and moved our possessions to Los Angeles. We made the cross-country trek because I was sick of the wretched weather in New Jersey and New York and Massachusetts. Wherever I had lived, the snow, the slush, the cold, the humidity—uhhgh—it never ceased to be intemperate outside. California seemed like just the climate I so desperately desired.

We were not disappointed. But we were also not prepared for the cultural gap that separated these two great cities (New York and Los Angeles).

In the northeast, creativity meant being pleasantly predictable. In the west, it meant being unique. In New York, you were able to get only as far as your pedigree allowed: your family name, your educational background, your list of contacts. In L.A., nobody seemed to care if you had attended college; your name was generally misspelled by the temporary help, anyway; and your contacts were probably in today and gone tomorrow, so that was only of passing help. The eastern capital emphasized rolling with tradition; the western point city focused upon creating new realities.

There is no doubt in my mind that if I had attempted, at the same tender age, to launch my research company in the heartland of the Establishment, I would have been extinguished like a forest fire—quickly and without sentiment. In L.A., my move was seen as a natural: clients had no problems accepting our fledgling firm as legitimate. (Let me give God His due in this miracle, too.)

Having lived in or just outside of six major cities across the nation has sensitized me to their idiosyncrasies. Conducting business in each of the major markets of the country has further sharpened my understanding of how they operate. Believe me, L.A. is not the laid back sun mecca it is portrayed to be. Neither is New York the economic nucleus that it may have been in days past.

But the key for those of us in full-time ministry may be to recognize just how drastically different the two coasts are in their life orientation. In terms of educational importance, entertainment values, financial perspectives, willingness to take creative risks, relationship and interpersonal attitudes, the importance of spiritual involvement, and views on leisure and work, much more than 3,000 miles separates our two dominant cities. If you have reason to reach out to people in such vastly divergent places, be cognizant of how unique and distinctive they truly are.

People

2

Lesson

Americans are world-class amnesiacs. We aren't so much forgiving as we are forgetful.

We had an international visitor to our home several years ago who liked to analyze the world. He was certain he had Americans figured out and was determined to exhibit his command of the American culture. We were arrogant, intelligent, hard-working, and aggressive. And, he contended, we were also a very forgiving people. Just witness what we had done to rebuild Germany and Japan, how we had forgiven so many debts from Third World countries, or how we continued to embrace most Europeans (except, perhaps, the French) in spite of how they typically thought of and treated us.

I believe he was right about the initial quartet of attributes. But he seriously blundered when he got to the one about being forgiving. Americans are probably no more or less forgiving than any other group of people. But

I maintain that we are much more forgetful than most other people.

Ask a person why Richard Nixon left office prematurely and you're liable to be asked who Richard Nixon was. (Remember, he's the one with the dog named Checkers.) Ask about the difficulties of Jimmy Carter's presidency and you're more likely to hear about his peanut farm or brother Billy's drinking than about the inflation-riddled economy or the hostage crisis of his term. I'd give you more examples but, being a pretty typical American, I can't recall any other significant examples...

There are some important implications of this chronic amnesia. For instance, when clergy ask me if the Swaggart and Bakker scandals have irreparably damaged the reputations of credible Christian ministries, the answer is "no." Why? Because most people have only a vague recollection of what those brouhahas were all about. At the time of those scandals, they were big news and many people questioned the credibility of televangelism, churches, preachers, the Bible, and anything even remotely related to the Christian faith. For a few months directly after each scandal, the image of Christianity and all sincere ministry endeavors took a beating.

But over the long haul, the statistics show that things have returned to normal. Most people have long since forgotten what happened. Who can retain the memory space needed for such old news when there are newer, fresher, more perverse, more unique or personally threatening scandals and crises in the public view?

The individuals most likely to recall the televangelist incidents and to make a continuing stink about them are the very individuals who had a thing against Christianity long before Swaggart and Bakker made the headlines. These Christian-bashers were on the prowl for anecdotal evidence to support their anti-Christian views. Brothers Jimmy and Jim simply provided the atypical but form-fitting facts that the anti-Christian polemic needed.

Given the short memories of the American people, the most strategic approach to major controversies is either to launch a full-on offensive that you know you will win or to simply wait for the noise to cease and the dust to settle. Depending on the people groups affected, and the amount of dust that needs to settle, history suggests that as long as new crises and media exposés are brewing, last year's scandal is likely to become little more than an occupational stepping stone for the journalist who broke the story. At least, that's the way most Americans will remember it.

Lesson

Americans are bombarded by increasing amounts of information, but are less well-informed about their world than ever.

American enterprise now churns out more data in a year than it used to in a decade. Computers can provide access to facts and figures within seconds that used to take literally days, if not weeks, to uncover. You can store and retrieve more information on a plastic disk five inches in diameter than you used to store in an entire set of encyclopedias. The media broadcast more information about current events to more people in a wider geographic band than ever.

And the typical American still doesn't have a clue who the Secretary of the Treasury is.

You've probably read the recent surveys and tests demonstrating how little both adults and children know about the world in which they live. Maps are a beautiful but baffling puzzle. Political leaders other than the president have a name recognition level equal to that of the players on the roster of the Sacramento Kings (let's see, is that baseball, basketball or football?). Insight into technology lapsed into the realm of the unconscious once we required people to get beyond the on/off switch of a Nintendo system.

All of this has weighed heavy on my heart. Not, mind you, because I fear for the soul of the nation once it loses its collective intelligence, but because I conduct research and write books. And who needs a writer or researcher when the average adult is still struggling with the process of setting the timer on their VCR?

But now that you mention it, the quest for cerebral gridlock has radically altered the way we have to communicate with people these days. For instance, I can't get away with simply displaying a data table anymore. Now it has to come with a picture (excuse me, a graphic element, as they say in the biz). It's no longer adequate to use overheads or handouts (of which I am abundantly guilty); now you have to show short, colorful, fast-moving videos to convey your point. And the most important part of the client reports we develop these days are not the conclusions but the summary.

In the Age of Information Overload, communication is a new process altogether. Different language (short words), new formats (graphics), fewer points. Sounds like it should be easier but for me, at least, giving less takes more.

Lesson

You only do a truly great job at those things you have been built to do.

I have finally given up trying to be the ultimate man-for-all-seasons-good-Samaritan.

When I was young, baseball teams generally kept a "utility player" on the roster. They were the guys who could play every position but were truly superb at none of them. Their value was the flexibility they lent their team in the case of an emergency. Need a first baseman? Bill's the guy. Did the shortstop get injured? Substitute Bill. You sent in a pinch-hitter for the left fielder and don't have anyone who can play that turf? Insert Bill. The catcher just got his shoulder rearranged on a play at the plate? Put the mask and pads on Bill.

But the utility player is an anachronism now. This is the age of specialization. As Charles Emerson Winchester, the Harvard-trained surgeon on the old TV series *M*A*S*H* once proclaimed, "I do one thing at a time, I do it well, and I do it at a reasonable pace." Or something like that...

Admittedly, I'm a quasi-renaissance man. I enjoy intensive involvement in sports, music, writing, reading, teaching, traveling, statistical noodling, and debating. And I've made the mistake of trying to spread myself so thin that I'm a transparent man. There is value to focusing and applying oneself to a specific arena in which you excel.

I think this may be part of the reason why so many business and church leaders struggle so much these days. Charged with responsibilities that far exceed their capabilities, they endeavor to accomplish things that are beyond their scope. Now, there is something to be said for being challenged, since such a stretch leads to personal growth. On the other hand, though, there's a danger that outweighs the potential benefit: doing many tasks poorly because you just don't have what it takes to do those tasks at the highest levels of performance.

Don't ever ask me to be a family or marriage counselor; I don't have the sensitivity and emotional complexion to be helpful. If, in a moment of ignorance or weakness, you ask me to host a reception or to create a warm social atmosphere, you'll pay the price.

I suppose only one Person really knows what I'm like, but I can probably get some deeper insight into who I really am if I really want to know. And the best use of that insight is to draw the boundaries for my involvement in life so that I am set up for successful and positive experiences, rather than venturing into danger zones which will almost certainly lead to emotional, psychological or spiritual hurt and misery.

As Peters and Waterman said more than decade ago, "stick to your knitting."

Lesson

You're either a thinker or a feeler.

For years I struggled with certain employees, trying to get them to do things my way. I'd enter the meeting with a well-defined, carefully-conceived plan for action (emphasis on *action*). They'd always want to talk at length about the plan and its elements, rather than get on with the project. There were many a day when I wanted to simply toss them out and bring in some people of depth.

To me, these touchy-feely types were molasses in the machinery. To them, I was a gruff and obstinate bully who was never interested in what they felt about the plans or why they felt that way. Ours was a classic case of the thinkers trying to manage the feelers without a clue as to the personality dynamics that were in place.

Being results-driven, since our company benefited from the performance of the feelers, they were not unceremoniously dismissed (as was often my burning desire). In retrospect, this was clearly the restraining hand of God at work, preventing BRG from getting bogged down with a bunch of Barna clones. (What a heartless—but efficient—machine that would be!) Over time, through reading, seminars, head-to-head confrontations with the feelers, conversations with superb managers, and the use of personality tests, I've learned a bit about the two groups and have even come so far as to appreciate feelers.

I could never have admitted this a few years ago, but now it seems obvious that us thinkers need some first-rate feelers to help round out our world. All thought and no sensitivity makes for a very nasty world. And the same can be said for feelers; running on emotion without true insight can cause some real problems.

Through some very tough times, God has helped me to understand that He made each of us differently and that my own shortcomings can be compensated for by the talents and skills of those whose lives I neither envy nor understand very well. Just as some feelers have expanded my personal and professional horizons, hopefully I, too, can add a new dimension to the lives of some feelers. The key is to blend our respective differences to arrive at a mutually beneficial outcome.

Seeing the thinker-feeler continuum for what it is has enabled me not only to work better with people (though I still have a long way to go), but also to do a better job at hiring people, placing them in an appropriate job, and providing learning opportunities that are significant for them. It's not a one-size-fits-all world when it comes to learning opportunities or occupational development strategies. And while I will never become a feeler, I can become a better thinker by understanding some aspects of the world of the feeler.

Honestly, I still am and always will be a thinker. My worst nightmare is being stuck on a desert island without books, a laptop computer—and to be surrounded by a dozen feelers. They'll probably want to hug me, then sit in a circle and share our inner-most feelings about our predicament so we can process the horror together. Mercy drowning, please!

But maybe it's a sign of growth that I believe even in that circumstance, those people will help me learn something new about myself, my circumstance, and my God. I'll probably hate the means, but appreciate the ends. And I'll only admit it to them grudgingly.

I think I feel better already.

Lesson

Everyone loves a gift.

I hate pretense. So when a salesman or supplier sends me a gift, I become suspicious. He's up to something underhanded. Maybe he's trying to soften me for a rate increase. Perhaps it's a subterfuge for an inferior product.

Well, that's the old George Barna at work. The new, improved version has learned that everyone loves to be loved. And if you use a prop to get that message across, that's okay.

It's a lesson that was not easily or quickly learned. It took one of my employees to teach me—the boss—the lesson.

We work for a variety of clients, some secular, some Christian. Our single, largest project each year is conducted on behalf of a secular consulting firm. Since the project does not require the types of skills that I bring to a project, I assigned the job to one of our project directors.

To make a long story short, she has maximized the supplier-client relationship. How? By simply befriending the contact people at the client organization in a very genuine way. She talks with them frequently, about job-related aspects and about non-job related aspects. They work well together because they have gotten to know and trust each other.

She has given them a unique gift: her caring.

It astounds me that sometimes I forget the importance of the relationship underlying the product. Part of the product is the client's confidence in me, as a person, not just as a researcher. If they do not get to know me as anything more than a technician, they may not have much trust in my capacity to take a deeper interest in who they are and what they are trying to achieve. And without that type of confidence built into the relationship, it's strictly a dollars-and-cents relationship. You can get that anywhere these days.

So I guess everyone likes to get a gift, now and then. And when the gift is not store bought, but is clearly authentic, what a difference it can make.

Leadership

3

Lesson

It's much easier to lead without vision, but it's virtually impossible to be successful or fulfilled that way.

There are tens of thousands of organizations in this country that are being led by people who have an idea, but no vision. Those are the organizations which will join the ranks of the bankrupt within the coming decade. It can almost be guaranteed.

Perhaps the most important concept I have studied over these last ten years, aside from my acceptance of Christ as Savior and all that decision has meant, has been the concept of vision. From my vantage point, it is the single quality that separates the men from the boys. You can launch an organization without it, but you really cannot get far without vision. And the more complex our society becomes, the more competitive the marketing environment gets, the more skeptical the people become—the less feasible it will be even to attempt to do anything of significance until the vision is in place.

Much of our political turmoil these days is a direct result of the lack of vision emanating from and directing the paths of our highest leaders. The Church is embroiled in in-fighting and plagued by a lack of cultural impact because few of its key power brokers and influencers have grasped God's vision for the Church today. We have more bankruptcies per thousand new businesses these days because the individuals taking the risks are often doing so with the force of energy, ego, creative ideas or greed, but rarely with a compelling vision to match.

There is really no substitute for strong leadership. A movement or organization without strong leadership is like a sports car without an engine. It may look formidable, but it doesn't have the guts to go anywhere. Vision is the "guts" of the leader.

Vision is tough work. Whether you are driven by the goal of making money through some type of manufacturing enterprise, of satiating the demands of customers in a service organization, or seeking to make truth comprehensible and applicable through a local church, vision is irreplaceable. But it requires a concentrated effort to distill it, a ferocious appetite to implement it, and the undying commitment to casting it to the people with whom you labor.

It's so much easier just to get a good idea and run with it. And the power of a good idea should not be underestimated. Some organizations got on their feet initially simply via the strength of a great idea. But after the excitement and passion spurred by the idea wear thin, there must be a core vision in place which will boost the organization forward. No vision, no long-standing means of growing the idea.

It's tempting simply to out-organize someone else who has a great idea. But structure and management, by themselves, do not spur anything lasting. They must be tied to the distinctive, compelling, strategic, long-term, focused, exciting, harmonizing, unchanging perspective that sets the organization apart on the basis of its heart, not its hierarchy. That is, unless you have a true vision to carry out, the best management practices and most well-designed organizational charts will serve no purpose and leave no imprint.

Leaders, too, invariably discover that unless they have a motivating vision for the future, simply producing more stuff to make more money loses its taste after a while. But chasing the vision for a better future—now *that* is something that can stimulate their thinking and their energy toward achieving something that is worthwhile.

Satisfaction may occur when goals and objectives are reached. But fulfillment is achieved when there is truly the hope or experience of turning the vision from dream to reality.

Lesson

If you want to get something done, give it to the busiest person—but only if you're not in a hurry.

The old adage says that the best way to get something done is to assign it not to the person who has nothing going on, but to the one who is already the busiest. The reasoning is that the busy person has already proven himself or herself. And since past performance is perhaps the best indicator of future productivity, your best shot is to run with the one who has already proven himself or herself.

There's only one fault with this reasoning. In today's society, there are so few individuals who have proven themselves to be capable of producing what is needed with the standard of quality required, they are no longer simply busy. They are overwhelmed.

These producers will probably (perhaps grudgingly) take on whatever additional special assignments you throw their way. And the chances are pretty good that they'll get what you want done. But given their workload, the chances may be good that they will not be able to get what you need done by the time you need it done.

So where does all this leave you?

If you're a good leader, you've already considered how this project fits within the scope of the organization's vision and have delegated the task to a suitable manager.

If you're a good manager, you've assigned the job to the appropriate employee and are giving that individual sufficient leeway so that they can own the job and reap the psychic rewards from their accomplishment.

If you're the prototypical reliable employee—the one who is always busy because somehow you get the job done—you've probably gone through the wailing and gnashing of teeth and agreed to do the task. At this moment, though, you're totally stressed out over the time frame associated with the project.

And if you're a typical Baby Buster employee, you probably don't even remember the assignment. When it's really needed, the boss will ask about it. At that point it will justify your attention.

So, *you* figure out where things are at, and where you'd like them to be. Just make sure you get a head start.

Lesson

Public opinion is usually soft. A real leader can shape it however he or she wants.

Have you ever wondered just who is telling the truth in the abortion debate regarding whether Americans believe abortion is a viable solution or not?

What about opinions related to the performance of the president, whoever he happens to be at any given moment? Have you ever seen numbers that bob up and down as rapidly as these measurements?

Have you paid attention to the public's opinions regarding issues such as divorce, the defense budget, the role of women in society, views on homosexuality, the separation of church and state, and caring for the elderly? There are more poll-supported positions on these issues than there are Baskin-Robbins flavors of ice cream.

How is it possible that public opinion seems to bounce around so much? Are the surveys themselves flawed? Are the statistics being reported erroneously?

The most likely truth is that on most issues, people do not know what they believe. One of the great tragedies of survey research is that if you ask people a question, they will give you an answer—whether they have an opinion or not. Sometimes, what we measure is what might be deemed *momentary opinion* or the *attitude of the day*. Lacking any depth of understanding or knowledge related to the issue at hand, the respondent will provide the interviewer with a valid reply. The reply gets tabulated, along with all the other more or less valid responses from other individuals. The result is the statistic that gets reported publicly.

Due to the lack of depth or true understanding possessed by the individual on the topic in question, it is common, if not entirely likely, that asking the same person the same question just one month later will derive a very different answer. It's not because the respondent is lying, but because they really don't know what they think, and thus provide the best answer they can at the moment the question is posed.

What is often more important to measure than the mere *direction* of response is the *intensity* with which the respondent clings to that answer. In the political campaigns I used to manage, we would market the candidate to people differently, depending upon the intensity of their candidate preference. It made for a much more logical allocation of our resources and made the messages we sent to likely voters much more meaningful, from their perspective.

Perhaps the biggest lesson I've learned regarding the softness of people's opinions on even the most significant issues of the day is that the public is yearning for leaders who can put structure and meaning to all of these issues. Vision, ideology, philosophy—call it what you will, but people are searching for strong leaders who will frame the questions of the day in such a way that the world once again makes sense.

Put differently, one of the marks of a strong leader is the willingness, the determination and the ability to direct people's opinions and attitudes in such a way as to provide them with a working worldview. Leaders are leaders precisely because of their ability to carry the masses in a specific direction. The great leaders can accomplish this without force because their ideas are so tightly knit, and the probable outcomes from the pre-scribed course of action is so compelling, that people are anxious to follow.

The lesson, though, is that public opinion is generally waiting to be shaped. The process requires a multi-stage strategy for challenging, explaining, persuading, and rein-forcing people's thoughts and decisions related to an issue or perspective.

The tension point here is to achieve the balance of recognizing that people are crying out for a clear perspec-tive and to be led somewhere important; while at the same time giving the people sufficient credit for being able to sense a phony, to see through baloney, and ulti-mately to make good decisions (collectively, at least).

If you are interested in leading people somewhere, it's important to take stock of their existing views and opinions. But realize that if you measure the intensity of those views, you'll find that most opinions on matters of culture, values, politics and religion are just like beauty: only skin deep.

Lesson

Bad outcomes are often attributable to bogus assumptions.

Which of these statements has intruded into your decision-making realm in the last few years?

- *"People always act in their own best interests."*

  Then explain why Los Angeles has always resisted a real mass transit system, or why the majority of incumbent Congressmen get re-elected, or why most people are not Christians.

- *"You cannot legislate morality."*

  Really? Then why do we have the Civil Rights Act? Why all the fuss over the Equal Rights Amendment? Isn't the underlying purpose of many laws the directing of people's behavior because we know that, left to their own devices, they'd act immorally?

- *"Baby Boomers are selfish people. They do not contribute money, even to causes they believe in."*

  In truth, the evidence shows that Boomers are rather generous, but they donate their money in ways that radically differ from previous generations.

These are just three common but silly expressions of contemporary thought that come to mind. They are statements based on bad information. They are unfounded assumptions. And unfounded assumptions are, I believe, one of the most widespread causes of disaster in organizations. Accepting and acting upon bad assumptions undermines many leaders.

I study churches more than other organizations, so let me consider the impact of bad assumptions on a typical church and its decision-making.

From square one, there are loads of bogus assumptions that flavor the decisions of churches. Try on a few of these and see if they fit your experience.

- *A pastor should be a seminary graduate. That is a minimum credential and demonstrates the individual's exposure to and mastery of church systems and theology.*

- *A friendly congregation will grow. It simply needs to have contact with visitors, and the natural openness of the existing congregation will attract newcomers and compel them to stay.*

- *If you pastor a church dominated by older people, you have to somehow shift their attention to reaching younger people. Otherwise, the older folks will die off or become incapacitated, and before you know it you'll be left with a small or immobile church.*

- *You can't change the traditions of the church. They provide a sense of comfort and security to the people. Trying to bring in new approaches will simply push people out the door.*

Where do these counterfeit perceptions of the real world come from? Sometimes it is simply from an honest misunderstanding of circumstances. Sometimes it is the result of focusing on the wrong data. Sometimes the problem is intentional deception, commonly known as "justification" or "rationalization." Whatever the source, it undermines our efforts to do our best.

The antidote that has worked best for me as I try to smoke out the bad assumptions in my own decision-making situations has been to constantly ask the question "why?" The beer commercial notwithstanding ("Why ask why?"), trying to ferret out all of my underlying assumptions and asking myself their genesis or what supporting data I have for those assumptions generally proves helpful.

I innocently buy into dozens of assumptions, based upon unreliable information or perspectives passed down to me from others who have unwittingly (usually) accepted and embraced the same indefensible values, beliefs and viewpoints. The damage of such a lack of circumspection can be (and, on various occasions, has been) devastating.

Next time somebody makes a blanket statement of fact or perspective, challenge their assumptions. It might save your neck later on.

Lesson

Arriving at a solution to most problems requires attention, not brilliance.

Many, if not most, of today's problems in business, family, personal relationships, government, and ministry are the result of neglect and sloppiness. Preoccupied with more alluring challenges, or failing to prioritize our resources properly, we make some decisions that will haunt us later. Naively, we often chalk these difficulties up to the complexity of the circumstances. Realistically, though, the genesis of the problem was that we failed to commit a sufficient share of our attention to the matter at the appropriate time.

In other words, many of the problems that consume us can be solved by simply assigning them sufficient attention. Brilliance needs to be trotted out only on rare occasion.

Think about the numerous decisions that you make in the course of a day. And then count up how many of those decisions are required because an appropriate decision or action was not made at the appropriate time. You may be surprised at how often our decisions are necessary only because we failed to divert enough attention to the situation in question at an earlier stage.

Anticipating problems is one means of avoiding the crisis management organization. In most cases, even a "crisis" is little more than putting out a brush fire. When the whole forest is on fire, then you truly have a crisis and a brilliant solution may be needed. But an organization that claims to exist on the basis of its ability to constantly and adroitly extinguish forest fires is either misrepresenting the magnitude of its fires or is on the edge of being extinguished itself. An organization cannot survive a crisis management mentality for any prolonged period of time.

If you are a leader, your best bet is to anticipate the scenarios that may emerge and have a ready answer. Some conditions will emerge without your anticipating them: that's when your attention is needed. Quickly. Decisively.

But brilliance? Don't waste it on the mundane daily tasks. Brilliance is a cherished commodity, which each of us can muster only on occasion; few can be brilliant on-demand. Lavish your brilliance on the bigger challenges of life, business and ministry that require such genius. And spend the rest of your time giving the necessary attention to the regular tasks and brush fires of your existing reality.

Lesson

The most powerful vacuum sucking time out of a leader's day is known as "meetings."

I don't like football. I avoid vegetables. But I detest meetings.

One of our clients is a multi-billion dollar corporation that is well-known to every air-breathing American. Having spent hundreds of hours inside their corporate apparatus, I have a working knowledge of what makes them tick. And I also have a strong conviction that if they sliced the number of meetings they call (and the number of hours involved) by half, they'd be a multi-*trillion* dollar corporation.

Churches are among the prime offenders in the Meeting Syndrome. Somehow we have confused two antithetical practices: ownership of the decision-making process and pointless discussion. For good reason, we seek to get the laity involved in the process of ministry by having them reflect and decide upon the factors that shape ministry. Unfortunately, this focus on process often leads to a meandering series of interactions in which time is wasted, energy is squandered, excitement for ministry is minimized, and leaders are stretched thinner than the evidence used to challenge the Clarence Thomas nomination.

My boiling point with meetings was reached a few years ago when I was an elder in a nearby church. They had a monthly elders meeting that began promptly anywhere between 6:30 and 7:00 and lasted until the individual with the highest tolerance for pain could stand no more. As luck would have it, apparently I was the one with the lowest threshold for pain and won the award for Most Fidgety Elder two years running.

After about six months of dutifully observing the process (after all, new elders are expected to attend, but it will take some time to truly grasp the nature of the calling), I came to a conclusion. The process did not work.

So, I came up with *Barna's Rule of Time Management.* "If we can't get this stuff done within two good hours of effort, it's probably not worth doing." In a series of private conversations, I let the leaders of the elder board know that at the two hour and one minute mark, I'd be leaving them, with best wishes for the rest of their meeting.

I was not a well-loved elder. But the meetings did get a bit shorter, I'm told, as others began to resent the fact that after just two hours of torture I was experiencing freedom.

There's more to the tale. I found the *Rule* to be so liberating that I started instituting it in the conduct of my business. Frankly, I haven't found many clients (and not a single employee) who have felt cheated because I refused to sit through anything more than two hours of meetings at a stretch.

I have never studied law, so I don't know the content of many of today's finest laws. But isn't this one of Murphy's Laws? *Meetings expand to consume the available time.* If it isn't, it should be.

Meetings are called for many unexpressed reasons. Some of those are laudable. But many of them are not. Reasons like internal politics. Loneliness. Weak leadership. Lack of ideas. Process paralysis. Tradition.

And a major cause of interminable meetings, or meetings in which there is no apparent direction, is the failure of the participants to prepare adequately for the ensuing discussion. Sometimes this is the fault of the convener, who failed to assign people appropriate responsibilities prior to the meeting. Sometimes it's because the participants were lazy or were the wrong people to be there in the first place. All of the participants suffer the consequences, regardless of where we lay the blame.

Meetings can be productive and valuable elements in the development of plans, in evaluations of performance, in the sparking of creative ideas, and in the effort to make meaningful decisions that will serve the corporate body well.

But use them judiciously. And, in your own best interests, never invite me to a meeting that lasts longer than two hours.

Lesson

Focus on the bad news.

It's only natural for us to concentrate on the good news. Profits are up, more people are coming to Christ, the building is paid for, the sermon was a hit. We work hard to make good things happen, and it is stimulating and pleasurable to discover that our efforts have had a positive impact.

The problem is, when we only focus on our successes, we lose sight of the problems that are lurking in the shadows, waiting to devour us and negate those successes.

If life were a static venture, we could ruminate on our achievements and revel in our victories. Life would be one big party. One of the biggest challenges we would face would be how to exceed the joy derived from past celebrations.

But life is dynamic, not static. Each victory we achieve restructures the world a bit, and creates a response to that change. And a victory in one dimension of our world does not protect us from threats and crises in other dimensions. To maintain our equilibrium and achieve on-going success, we must be alert to factors that demand attention or change.

It's hard for some people to acknowledge that there is a downside to life. You probably know some individuals who try to put a favorable spin on everything, as if to convince not just you, but also themselves, that things just could not be any better. To them it is as if admitting the existence of problems or challenges is an admission of guilt, failure, inattentiveness, or inability.

It's not. It's simply dealing with reality. Seeing the positive side of reality is good, but it needs to be balanced with an objective perspective of the circumstances.

My involvement with a wide range of non-profits, for-profits, and churches has shown me that one common characteristic of successful executives is that they spend their time digging for problems even while they celebrate their victories. They don't have to dig for success stories, because their organizations are filled with people who gravitate toward, cling to, and make waves about whatever is going well.

Leaders publicly champion those gains, too. The media portraits we gain of most leaders are when they are trumpeting some major step forward by their organization. But true leaders tend not to get overly emotional about those gains because they know that there is usually an unnoticed or intentionally hidden problem waiting to rear it's ugly head at the most inopportune moment. They spend most of their private, behind-the-scenes time exploring the depths of their corporate world to identify the next challenge that will require a tough decision, a new strategy or a greater investment of resources.

These executives are fascinating because they have somehow learned how to savor a victory at the same time that they are engaged in detecting a potential landmine. Internally they have installed (and triggered) some kind of balance mechanism that allows them to celebrate that which has worked without slackening their effort or attention in ways that will undermine the potential for having reasons to celebrate in the future.

We all need to feel the satisfaction or fulfillment of a job well done. Rewards are important in life. But leaders know that a changing environment brings new challenges that demand attention, even when a celebration over past successes is in full swing.

Lesson

Committees and task forces are usually a cover-up for weak leadership.

If you want to lead, you have to be willing to make the tough stands and to be opposed for your controversial decisions.

I cringe when I hear of an organization sending an item to be studied by a committee, or that a task force is being established to look into the matter. Yes, there are times when additional research is required before a proper decision can be rendered. But since when do committees and task forces churn out better information than a dedicated, capable individual assigned to the matter?

I am impressed by leaders who examine an issue, come clean by admitting they don't know what to do, and promise an answer will be rendered in a short, identified period of time. Forget the science of covering your anatomy by having a team of people whose research or recommendations you can point to if the decision turns sour. A leader accepts the challenge head-on and only uses task forces and committees to bury those items which ought not to have even made the agenda in the first place.

Here's a challenge. Study the activity of your organization during the past two years. How many times have you sent items requiring a decision "back to committee," or developed an "ad hoc" group to study the matter, or designated a task force to render its thoughts on the issue?

Was that action really necessary? Was it truly productive? To what extent did that procedure really enhance your decision-making ability?

Lesson

A great leader is an individual who accomplishes his or her own agenda without alienating those whose agendas were superseded.

Everyone has his or her own agenda when dealing with a leader. The great leaders are the ones who are able to quickly and silently figure out each person's agenda, and work around those motives to get them excited about the leader's agenda.

Now, there's a basic assumption built into this perspective, namely, that the leader *has* an agenda. "Agenda" is one of those words that has taken a beating over the years. It is usually associated with manipulation and scurrilous behind-the-scenes activity. I can imagine Harvey

Mackay's next book being titled *Beware the Well-Dressed Leader Who Has an Agenda.*

Let me speak up on behalf of agendas. It's okay to have an agenda. In fact, a leader without an agenda is like a pilot without a flight plan. He or she will move ahead, but nobody knows the final destination (although the pessimists in the crowd can predict the final outcome fairly accurately).

Back to the original train of thought. For most adults, their agenda is like their brand of Christianity: considered necessary, but not necessarily important. Knowing this enables a leader to help people reshape their agendas for a greater purpose.

Consider how two very different types of leaders handle a situation of conflicting agendas. First, there is the vision-driven leader. This leader works within the scope of the vision of the organization, sharing his or her view of how a different course of action than that espoused in others' agendas would achieve a more direct, more expansive payoff. This leader defeats the inner temptation to focus on the personal achievement associated with his or her agenda, or on the pursuit of pet projects, or on the challenge of winning the agenda debate. Instead, the emphasis is upon how pursuit of his or her agenda actually is a total "win" situation: every involved party winds up better off and the organization emerges victorious because the actions pursued are in line with its vision. There is no strong-arming or intense politicking because the force of a great idea that has been well-communicated is sufficient to bring everyone to the same conclusion: implement the leader's agenda.

The power-driven leader takes a very different path to seeing his or her agenda become reality. The game is perceived to be one of maximized manipulation: whoever can pull the most strings, exert the most pressure, or espouse the most clever argument wins the game. The objective here is not what is best for the organization or for the people involved, but to show that the leader in is control and can flex his or her decision-making muscle whenever needed.

Once again, the primary difference between a real leader and a titular leader is the application of vision. Possessing it is, in itself, not enough. An effective leader is one who can bring others along for the ride to victory by having first thought through the long-term implications and applications of the vision and who is capable of sharing that view of a better future with others who would benefit from, and could bring benefit to, others via the commitment to such a vision.

Lesson

Leaders do their homework.

One of the things that always impressed me about really effective leaders was that they seemed so smart. Whatever question came up in a meeting, whatever curve balls were thrown at them in a presentation, they always had just the right answer at their fingertips. I hoped that someday I, too, would be able to be such a sharp leader.

But as I became more friendly with some leaders, and had the chance to study the habits of others, their secret was revealed to me. It wasn't so much that they were unusually intelligent as that they were extraordinarily well-prepared.

Great leaders do their homework before stepping out of the office. They envision what the final goal looks like and work backwards to figure out how to get there. They imagine the questions they will be asked by others and conceive a reasonable response in advance. They study their colleagues, their competitors and their employees to identify their strengths, weaknesses and idiosyncrasies.

And they strategically determine what they must do to maximize their interaction with or in opposition to those individuals.

These leaders do not necessarily possess a photographic memory, nor are they necessarily the smoothest operators or most eloquent speakers. More often, they are simply the individuals who are so well-focused that they are ready for anything, at any given moment. The risks they take are well-calculated. The stands they take are never spur-of-the-moment. The challenges they throw out to others are done for a reason. They may not have the most reputable degrees, the fanciest offices or the highest public profiles. They are too busy getting the job done and getting ready for the next challenge to worry about such peripherals.

A few church leaders have added a unique twist to this preparedness: vulnerability. I've watched some pastors deflect both criticism and challenges by simply admitting to mistakes or ignorance. Yet, this only seems to be an effective response when they are sufficiently ready to substantively address the vast majority of questions or challenges. Only then does their vulnerability stand in vivid contrast to their more polished or pre-conceived remarks. And for vulnerability to really make an impact, it has to be authentic. I do not recall ever seeing a leader use vulnerability effectively when it was just a scripted, well-acted response.

No matter who the leader is, or what their training may be, or how well resourced their office is, being ready for all circumstances that might arise is tough, tough work. I've discovered that to be well-prepared and to use that resource in a leadership capacity, you have to deeply covet the privilege of leading people. Managing or simply inciting people is much easier, because those activities revolve around a less sophisticated, less intense set of skills. Leading takes a lot of time, effort and cerebral firepower to do well.

In the first ad agency at which I worked, I was fortunate to work closely with a man who fancied himself a first-class leader. It turns out that events proved his self-assessment to be a bit lofty, but I learned from his inadequacies.

I had worked hard to set up a major presentation for our firm. We flew into another city, and went directly to the hotel at which we met with the CEOs from five major organizations whose media accounts we wished to handle. My boss did his presentation, smoothly explaining our qualifications, our vision for the project, and how we could help these organizations grow. I was impressed. The man had done his homework.

Or so I thought. Once he was done with his portion of the presentation, the CEOs asked some pretty rugged questions. In retrospect, their questions were not so much unpredictable as they were solid, what-can-you-do-for-me-that-nobody-else-can inquiries. My boss started out strong but eventually wilted under the pressure of their scrutiny into his motives, his concepts and his understanding of their needs. He had done only a portion of his homework.

Had he done the full exploration of his assignment I am confident he could have won them all over. But, having arrogantly assumed that he could either out-think them or simply persuade them by force of character to follow his lead, he lost his bid to get the project off the ground.

Think about what you must study to be ready for the firing line. There are the issues which relate to the nature of your job; you must know your business inside out, and be able to deal with a very broad range of queries regarding the past, present and future of that business. There are factors related to people. Those insights must be handled deftly and delicately, but with sufficient authority to demonstrate leadership. There are elements related to opportunities that may not have arisen yet. There are challenges related to the vision for the organization, and how to integrate existing realities with that view of the future, both long-term and short-term. And there is the necessity of thinking through strategic challenges, counter-arguments, and personal matters, all of which may relate even tangentially to the decision-making procedures of the organization.

This is no small list of elements to juggle. Not everyone can do their homework quickly enough and well enough to do a superlative job as a leader. But the leaders who are making a difference in their own spheres of influence typically have accepted the challenge to do their homework. They get not just an "A" for effort, but also for performance.

Lesson

If you want it done right, do it yourself. If you want to maximize your impact, delegate the task.

Jimmy Carter vs. Ronald Reagan. Classic contrasts in leadership style.

Carter was the very intelligent, perfectionistic president who got totally bogged down in the details of the office. His presidency suffered many problems, not the least of which was his inability to adequately delegate many of those details to capable, trusted advisers and managers.

Reagan was the president whose intelligence was constantly criticized, and whose grasp of the details was reputedly minimal. His presidency suffered many foibles, too, but the delegation of important tasks was not one of those downfalls.

Who achieved more of their vision while in office, Carter or Reagan? Regardless of your feelings for these two men, an objective assessment of their presidential legacies indicates that Reagan wins that one, hands down.

I struggle from the same weaknesses that plagued Carter. I am blessed with the ability to handle a million details well, and to enjoy the little things. My tendency is to shoulder more of the load than a CEO (or pastor, or president, or chairman) ought to. Mastering a task thoroughly, which includes dealing with the range of details, can bring me a thrill.

But mastering the details detracts from the ability (if one has it) of seeing and pursuing the big picture with any degree of success. It is the rare person who can satisfactorily balance both the details and the grand view, and adequately make both realms happen. Most people have to commit to one or the other.

I think this is why it's so hard for many small churches to grow. The pastor is generally expected to be both the visionary (i.e. big picture) and the day-to-day operations director (i.e. details person). Trying to make both ends of the continuum work excellently, through the efforts of a single person, is nigh impossible. Similarly, most one-person companies struggle and usually go belly-up because one individual cannot proficiently complete the tasks of the visionary and the functionary simultaneously.

Most people are gifted at dealing either with the big picture or the details. Few can handle both sides equally well. If you are one of those gifted individuals, my discovery has been that you eventually have to make a choice; you must either become the leader who delegates in order to maximize impact or become the hands-on producer who sacrifices a focus on the big picture to make sure that the component activities are done just right.

Neither person can exist for very long without the assistance and support of the other. Strive to figure out which person you really are, to celebrate that uniqueness, and to team with someone whose skills and talents will complement your own. You'll save yourself a lot of agony by not trying to personally fill every position on the team.

Lesson

Making it on your own is satisfying. Experiencing that success with a true partner, though, is fulfilling.

No, this section is not written simply to appease my wife.

When I started the Barna Research Group, there wasn't really a "group" to speak of. I began as a one-man shop. (Well, one-man and one-dog, to be honest. Within less than a year, we grew to be a one-man, *two*-dog organization.)

I answered the phone, typed the letters, stamped the mail, wrote the proposals, called prospective clients, did presentations, created the invoices, etc. If it came from the Barna Research Group (BRG), it came from me.

Fortunately, one month into the company's existence, a friend who was the manager of research at The Disney Channel called and asked me if I'd be interested in doing some of Disney's research. After thinking for about a millisecond, I indicated that I could probably squeeze Disney into my schedule. That business relationship flourished, and eventually BRG became the primary research arm for the Channel. A new era for BRG had dawned: employees were added, equipment was purchased, space was rented, and amazingly, a profit was made.

The rapid growth was absolutely God's provision; I would never have had the nerve to ask a corporation with the name of Disney if I could do any of their work. While there were days when I supposed that working with the Mouse folks was God's punishment for some awful sins I must have committed, the BRG-Disney connection lasted for a number of years and facilitated our movement into our current focus upon the Church. If there is any glory to be gained in this process, it all goes to Him.

But the BRG-Disney partnership also enabled my wife to quit her previous job and join BRG full-time. She has been a tremendous blessing to the firm as it has alternately experienced spurts of growth and periods of contraction over the years. Without her keen insights, her heart to support me, and her special talents, we would never have made it to where we are today. Granted, this is not a world class rags-to-riches story. BRG remains (partially by design) a small, occasionally struggling company. Nevertheless, we are apparently achieving some impact within our target market and are enjoying the process of being used by God in unusual and unexpected ways.

The greatest benefit of having my wife involved, though, has been the ability to share the highs and the lows with a partner. I am an extreme introvert, but I cherish the opportunity to share my life with the few individuals with whom I closely bond. Going through the numerous trials and tribulations of growing an under-funded start-up company has been much easier and more fulfilling by having a hard-working, vision-sharing confidante waltzing through the trials with me. (The fact that my partner has been my wife has certainly been a boon for our marriage, too.)

I have been involved in other partnerships and can tell you first-hand that unless you have the right blend of personalities, vision and skills, a partnership can be the death of you. Rather than wringing joy from the highs and softening the lows, an unbalanced partnership seems only to magnify the lows. And, due to the imbalance itself, there are more of those lows to be magnified.

If you can achieve a great partnership, it's better than going solo. It makes the highs higher and the lows bearable. If you cannot find a great partner, think carefully before starting a business or taking on major responsibilities within one. It could be more than you're able to handle.

Religion
and
Church
Life

Lesson

Hindsight, as a tool for recognizing and comprehending God's grace, power and purposes, is under-rated.

All right, I'll admit it. I generally fail to recognize God's mighty hand at work in my life at the time in which He is doing something significant. Generally, some time must pass before I can look over my shoulder and see how things have changed, and how some really wonderful transformations have occurred not because of my own brilliance, but because of His power and love.

For some reason, we frequently dismiss such a historical discovery process as unsophisticated. Yet, such a characterization itself smacks of lack of depth and sophistication. What could be more fruitful and intelligent, the essence of wisdom, than learning from one's experience and redirecting our future course of actions as a result of what we discover God to be up to in our lives?

I typically spend my time trying to anticipate what the future will be like so that we can prepare wise responses to those conditions, and perhaps even play a key role in the shaping of the future through our sensitivity to the development of events. Yet, one of the best predictors of the future is an understanding of the past. As we learn from what God has done to and through us in prior circumstances, we can develop greater confidence in our and in His ability to create a better person (i.e. us) and a better world in which to live.

What this boils down to, I suppose, is encouraging people to take time not just to look into the future, but also to look into the past, to recognize how God has worked in our lives. Such insight would help us know what the future might hold, and how we might see God's hand in our lives. And it might also enhance our understanding of who He is, how He operates, and what He desires of us. Not a bad series of insights to gain.

Lesson

Maybe more people would read the Bible if they didn't already know "whodunnit."

When people already know who has won a football game that is broadcast on tape delay, they are less likely to watch it than when they are not sure of the outcome.

Prime time television programming that is re-run almost always earns a lower viewer rating than the first time the program was aired.

The typical adult will refuse to re-read a book they have already read in the past, choosing instead either to read a book they have never read or to spend their time doing something else.

Few adults return to theatres a second or third time to watch a movie they have already seen. And the chances of their renting the movie on video when it is released is greatly diminished; generally, people will rent a film they have never seen before.

Which leads us to the Bible. (I wish this discussion—or anything, for that matter—led *more* people to the Bible!) Do you think it's possible that most people do not read the Bible because they think they already know the story?

When you ask people about the Bible—its content, its real-life value—the responses are rarely short of amazing. People often note that they "know" the Bible—you know, it's that book about God, and Adam and Eve, and Jesus and the cross, and the Devil. They'll claim that they understand the theme: be good. And they suggest that they really do not need to re-examine its content because they are already familiar with the story line. Good triumphs over evil, God defeats the Devil, Jesus loves people, the apostles start some churches.

Few people really accept the Bible as a guidebook for daily life. Few truly believe that the Bible is the only book that imparts absolute truth about all aspects of life. Few people actually understand how all of the content fits together to help outline a viable worldview that can make life a simpler, more fulfilling, holistic experience.

In our entertainment-driven culture, people are fearful of boredom. No one wants to re-read the same old stories, few people want to retrace the plot of movies they've already seen, and nobody I know is interested in reading last week's newspaper again. We're in a culture that demands something novel and fresh, everyday. The Bible has such material. The best writers in the world labored for years to craft these stories. Then the Council of Carthage convened to pull together the "best of" into the canon. And most Americans have yet to be exposed to all the great little stories that make the Book so fascinating and so fruitful. (Not to mention God's command that we know Him, which means knowing His Word.)

I think our task is not just to teach and preach theologically sound concepts, but to get people excited about the Word. This means making it relevant to them. This is a failing of most churches, according to the people who visit or regularly attend those churches. Granted, no church I've ever encountered wants to make the Bible *ir*relevant to people, but being committed to making it pertinent to what people really struggle with is altogether different.

Perhaps if we identify the felt needs that drive people's thoughts and behavior everyday we could figure out how to make the Bible seem like a valuable read. We don't have to compromise its content to seize people's attention with the life-changing insights it has to offer. But it will definitely take a decision to make the Word come alive for people who think they already know all they need to know from the pages of Scripture. Teaching the Bible the same old way we've been doing it for decades obviously doesn't cut it for millions of today's people—even though the Book itself has all the answers they're looking for.

Lesson

Most churches do not grow numerically because they do not want to grow numerically.

I think the most profound truths are those which are the most obvious and the most simple. Unfortunately, for me, at least, they are also the easiest to overlook.

One of those is that a church will only grow if the people of the church have clearly and generally established the will to grow as one of their driving passions. Not many churches experience swelling numbers of people when the core congregation is disgruntled about that expansion. As a people-based organization, a church grows in accordance to the spirit of the existing body.

This has been a useful, but hard realization for me. When I first got involved in the study of church growth, given my marketing background, I was quite excited about the natural application of basic marketing principles to the work and purposes of the Church. Not being a theologian by training, I was thankful that God would allow even a methodologist to have something to offer to the development of His Church.

Yet, somehow I overlooked the most basic principle of church growth, one which does not get spoken of or focused upon much. If the people want the church to grow numerically, it has a fighting chance. If the people do not yearn for such growth, it will be virtually impossible for numerical growth to occur.

Talk about a "back to basics" lesson! All too often I attempt to start running before I've studied the mechanics of walking. And I fear that many churches are similarly short-sighted. They apply all the growth principles and employ all the marketing techniques, but forget one necessary precursor: the people must have the hots for numerical growth. Without that ardent desire, they will not make the necessary sacrifices, will not pursue the appropriate means of expansion, and will not exhibit the attitude and heart of love and acceptance that must be in place if visitors are to stay at a new church.

If numerical growth is a key goal for your church, do not overlook the fundamental building block in the process. Your people must be excited about growing, they must be committed to such growth, and they must build their thinking, programs and efforts around such a goal.

Lesson

Some Christians are more interested in "serving" in ways that are personally comfortable than in doing whatever it takes to build God's kingdom.

Times have changed since our existing models for ministry were first developed and implemented. People's needs and expectations are different. Society's laws and technologies are different. The world's definitions of success, enjoyment and even religion are different.

So why is it that we keep coming back to the same strategies for reaching people that were used hundreds of years ago and show little return on the investment made, even though there are new options available to us which hold a reasonable potential for impact?

And why is it that so many people get in a religious rut when it comes to outreach and nurturing, and are not even willing to entertain the possibility that different, unusual approaches—ones that they, personally might not have responded favorably to—might have a greatly positive influence on others?

A pet peeve of mine is our inexplicable reluctance to use contemporary Christian music (CCM) as a means of attracting non-believers and as a means of encouraging, challenging and teaching believers. This is especially frustrating given our weak corporate experience in evangelism, the reality that Americans are most likely to accept Christ before they reach the age of 18, and the well-documented impact of music upon the lifestyles and values of people.

Why do we so stubbornly reject CCM as a growth and evangelism tool? From what I've been able to determine it is partially a response to the "rock music is of the Devil" philosophy; partially because so many pastors and church leaders are older and cannot really relate to the music of younger people; partly a consequence of seminaries training pastors to think that it is their preaching that saves people, and their home visitation practices that make the Bible clear.

CCM is not going to bring every non-believer to their knees in response to God's grace. But neither does preaching. Neither does choir music. Neither do Sunday school classes. Neither do altar calls. The beauty of having a myriad of tactics available for expressing the Gospel is that there is a means of sharing the Gospel that is tailor-made for every person.

The real question is, are we willing to set aside our own petty preferences long enough to let God work through a variety of means to connect with those who are searching for Him? After all, whose kingdom are we trying to build: ours or His?

Lesson

Failure repeats itself if you let it.

Did you know that the divorce rate among people who have been divorced and remarried is actually higher than among those who have been married just once?

Did you know that individuals who have been imprisoned in the past are many times more likely to get arrested and returned to prison than is the average person who has never been imprisoned?

We've all heard that history repeats itself. You've probably experienced it in your own life.

But have you stopped to recognize that the Church in America, today, is just as prone to repeating the same miscues and foibles as is any person you know? Isn't that discouraging? We can actually predict, with a high level of accuracy, how frustrated the organized Church will be in its efforts to be the salt and light of the nation in the coming decade by simply reviewing what we have done in the past decade.

As I have studied the present-day American Church and its multifarious elements, the likely repetition of avoidable mistakes seems, well, unavoidable. Unavoidable, that is, unless we commit ourselves to consciously and intentionally breaking the pattern of dysfunctional behavior and chart a new course for tomorrow.

Why the pessimism? Seminaries encourage the long life of our mistaken ways by continuing to teach leaders to perform the same functions in the same ways, regardless of the changes in the culture they serve. The people in our churches are allowed to resist change. Rare is the church leader who embarks on a journey designed to lead the people into the comprehension and acceptance of change. And perhaps as much as, if not more than, any other nation, we have encouraged the people in our churches to custom build a spiritual comfort zone around themselves, a bubble which cannot be burst without considerable effort.

The reason why I write books and articles which tend to put a different spin on our view of reality is because we cannot hope to break free from the patterns and ruts that bind us if we are not willing to experience reality from a different perspective. It is so intriguing to encounter people, especially pastors, who reject the things I write because it does not confirm what they believe.

Hey, the purpose of analyzing culture and attempting to explore varying interpretations of that culture is not to distill reality into neat little balls of truth that can be mass produced and easily marketed for everyone's pleasure. The purpose is to kick-start people's brains, inciting them to consider a novel understanding of *other* people's realities, hopefully leading to a more creative and impactful response to existing circumstances.

A good friend of mine speaks to church audiences and loves to pepper his presentations with one-liners. One of his "gems" that has stuck in my mind is: "nothing changes if nothing changes." I don't know if he originated that one, but he's on target. Until you and I resolve to alter our circumstances, they will remain unaltered. And until we determine that the ways in which we make God real to people are in need of re-evaluation and redesign, the chances of repeating the same errors and tragedies that are currently confounding our ministries are great indeed.

Lesson

Too many churches treasure order more than impact.

Talk to church leaders. Have them describe what they think they really want for their church. Usually, you'll get answers that revolve around impact.

But then observe what really happens at the church. You'll probably see an institution which is more aggressively pursuing order than impact. This is not done out of a spirit of conscious deception or manipulation. More likely, the condition has arisen without the leaders of the church even being aware of the reality. Over time, their views of stated intent and actual performance have become clouded.

Some of our recent research has confirmed the disharmony between word and deed. In fact, based on a blend of research and on-site observation of church behavior and pastoral leadership, I would offer the following for your consideration:

- Through our interviews, I've learned that more pastors are able to recite statistics related to attendance at services, dollars received, number of Sunday school classes, the length of last week's sermon and how many visitors attend on Sunday mornings than are able to provide a good estimate of how many people have accepted Christ as Savior in the past year in relation to some element of the church's ministry. These are factors that relate to order and predictability, rather than impact and life change.

- Pastors feel more comfortable giving staff and volunteers titles than they do merely assigning responsibilities and authority without a sense of position and hierarchies. Why? Because that way everyone has his or her place and his or her domain of activity. Clarity of position and internal organizational status supersedes concentration upon productivity.

- Church leaders retain a considerable degree of faith in Sunday school as both an educational and evangelistic vehicle, despite statistics that undermine that view. They are less comfortable with special events, often because of the potential for unforeseen circumstances or unpredictable outcomes.

- When asked to choose between two alternatives in the area of programs, pastors typically opt for the most conservative, lowest risk option. This is a reflection of the underlying view that you're better off maintaining the status quo than risking a temporary setback. In other words, continuity is superior to potential transformation because the potential cannot be guaranteed.

- Many churches continue to push for door-to-door, cold-call evangelism even though their own evidence overwhelmingly indicates that the method does not work. But relational evangelism, an amorphous, impossible-to-manage approach to building the church, is seen as less acceptable because it lacks structure and central control.

I'm not seeking to pass judgment on the theology of any church group, or to make unwarranted criticisms of the ways in which a church structures its services, its programs, or its ministry activities. Ministry is hard work, and the outcomes are never completely predictable or 100% satisfying, no matter how well-planned, well-funded or well-attended. Church leaders need all the help and every advantage they can get, and if utilizing structure and order, even in sometimes Byzantine or archaic forms, is truly efficient or productive, go for it.

What I *am* interested in doing is recognizing that sometimes we get so focused on developing a well-defined, highly ritualized, polished organization that we forget our real purpose in being the Church.

Order and structure are not merely good or useful; they are necessary components of a healthy, functional church. But when we allow the means to overshadow the end, we have a problem.

And I'm sure we agree that ours is a God of order, a God who hates confusion. But He is the same God who has called us to touch people's lives for His higher purposes. I cannot imagine Him accepting our lame excuses about statistics, order, hierarchies, guaranteed outcomes and lines of authority as plausible substitutes for getting the *real* job accomplished.

Where your treasure is, there, too, will your heart be. When you perform an intensive, objective assessment of how *your* church is conducting itself, where is its heart?

Lesson

Quantity is much more appealing than quality.

How many churches do you know that have true measures of the quality of their ministry, and doggedly take and analyze those measures? Compare that against the number of churches you know who measure the quantitative aspects of their ministry. It's an embarrassing comparison.

America remains committed to the philosophy that bigger *is* better. Oh, it's not sexy to come right out and admit that's how we feel, but we feel it nevertheless. And if you can get some high quality thrown in for good measure, well, then you've beaten the system.

One of the strategies of the Church that has driven this point home for me is the burgeoning church planting movement. I believe that planting churches is a superb evangelistic and spiritual growth tactic. I have been involved in the planting of several churches, and while I would *not* highly recommend it as a fun exercise (it has its moments, but they tend to be few and far between in the early stages of the initiation), such churches do possess greater evangelistic potential than the average church that is more than 20 years old.

Many denominations have set church planting goals to be reached by the year 2000. "1000 more by '94." "2000 in 2000." You've undoubtedly heard the themes associated with the numerical goals set by the denominations.

Here's what I don't understand. *If* the goal is to create churches that thrive because the people are really passionate about Jesus and about serving Him, and *if* we want to use our limited resources effectively in building His kingdom, and *if* we are attempting to demonstrate integrity in our efforts for His glory, then *why* don't we at the same time we plant a new church nail the doors shut of one that is dead? These dead churches merely siphon off funds, energy, people, and spiritual vigor that could be used more productively elsewhere.

I think the reason why is related to elementary mathematics. For each church we acknowledge to be dead, and then actually shut down, we have to plant *two* new churches in its place to move us one church closer to reaching the pre-determined numerical goal by the pre-determined date. In other words, attending to the *quality* of churches and using standards for spiritual vitality as the justification for a church's continuation, we might actually double the church planting requirement. This would not be (and, to every denominational leader I've mentioned it to, has not been) a popular notion.

What makes this all the more amazing is that the two key numbers on which so much of the intra-denomination planting fervor is based—i.e. the year 2000 and the number of new churches to be initiated—are relatively random. They have no scriptural basis and no statistical validity, yet they create all manner of hustle and bustle as we seek to fulfill these meaningless figures.

Anyway, please think about this. How do you measure the *quality* of your ministry? How do you connect the quality level with the quantitative growth associated with your ministry? How can each form of growth inform the other so that a synergistic impact is achieved?

It is certainly to our detriment that we focus solely on quantitative growth. You can have numerical growth in spite of sub-par quality. But I have yet to see a church that fails to realize quantitative increases in spite of top-notch quality. Maybe we cannot determine if the chicken or the egg came first, but I think we can ascertain that quality ought to precede quantity when it comes to building a true community of believers.

Lesson

Citing 'lack of funds' is a common smokescreen that hides the real problems of a ministry.

"If we only had the money, we could make this church *happen.*"

I doubt it.

Money is rarely the real problem in ministry. People, Christian people primarily, really get excited about effective ministry. It's such a novelty. And everybody likes to feel like they are part owners of something that is unique and effective.

No, money is not really the problem. A leader's attitude about money may be the stumbling block. Most likely, the lack of vision, plans, and all-out commitment to serving Him is the real problem.

Money is given in response to God's vision for the ministry which the leader is dead-set on implementing with absolutely the highest quality of performance.

Money is given when people see sufficient, tangible evidence of real leadership, when decisions are made intelligently and timely, when people are integrated into the flow of the ministry according to their interests and talents, and when direction, evaluation, and encouragement are provided. Money is given to a ministry when it stands a realistic hope of making a discernable difference in the world.

Money is rarely the root problem. Americans give more than $50 billion a year to religious activities that take place right here in America. That's a lot of money. And it's plenty to sustain a movement that is at its most formidable when it is lay-driven, relationship-oriented, and not tied to bricks-and-mortar obligations.

Money is not the problem.

Lesson

We use a secret language that communicates clearly.

What is the functional purpose of the local church? A key purpose is to communicate, in clear and relevant terms, what the Christian Church is all about.

We do that very effectively. Unfortunately, I don't believe we are doing it in quite the way we intend.

Please tape record your Sunday morning service this week. Listen to the words that are used. If your church is typical, you employ a secret language. I say "secret" only because there are no overt training courses on how to speak or interpret the language, no dictionaries that decipher the meaning of the words and expressions that comprise the language, and there is no official name for the language—no widespread acknowledgment that the language even exists.

But its' there.

Let's call this language "Christianese." Or maybe "Church-speak." Here are a few of the most common words and phrases that are employed by those who speak this secret tongue.

lift up to the Lord

prayer warriors

Christian walk

a word of prayer

the lost

get into the Word

giant of the faith

grounded in Scripture

prepare our hearts

fellowship

devout Christian

Can't you just hear a non-believer, visiting your church, struggling to make sense of our jargon-filled, bet-you-can't-penetrate-this language?

Is the following scenario, in which a visitor in the pews provides his church-member friend with a running, whispered commentary of his experience, so far-fetched?

PASTOR: Today, many are here with heavy hearts.

VISITOR: Don't they know about fat-free, non-cholesterol diets? Join a health club; eat less red meat.

PASTOR: What a privilege it is to lift you up to the Lord.

VISITOR: What, is this guy a power lifter, too? Man, his arms don't look that long, not long enough to lift them all the way up to God, anyway.

PASTOR: Let us say a word of prayer. Oh gracious and loving Father in Heaven,...[three minutes later]...for we ask these things in the name of your blessed Son, Jesus Christ. Amen.

VISITOR: Well, that was certainly more than "a word" of prayer, wouldn't you say?

PASTOR: How wonderful it is to be a prayer warrior.

VISITOR: Sounds like an oxymoron to me. Prayer warrior. Kind of like jumbo shrimp.

PASTOR: Today, I want to focus on your Christian walk.

VISITOR: What's that? A new rap dance?

PASTOR: As we get ready to dive into His Word, prepare your hearts.

VISITOR: Prepare my heart? What is this, the pre-op room?

PASTOR: Let's read from Ephesians, written by the apostle Paul. He was truly one of the giants of the faith.

VISITOR: What was he, about 6'6"? Maybe a 7-footer?

PASTOR: In this passage, Paul exhorts us all to be grounded in Scripture.

VISITOR: Whew, now that's definitely painful. I'm warning ya, this guy's not gonna ground me into anything.

PASTOR: Notice that Paul tells us...[30 minutes and many whispered perplexities later]...and so, if you are among the lost that are here today—

VISITOR: What kind of idiot could be lost here? We're in church, corner of First and Broadway, in Glendale.

Season your speech with enough of these words and expressions and you might as well be speaking in tongues, from the perspective of a non-Christian or a Christian who is not "mature" enough in the secret ways of the Church to have a clue as to your message.

Maybe this comes across as a bit humorous. Sadly, the use of such language is no laughing matter. The use of Church-speak communicates very clearly to those who are outsiders looking in. What it communicates is this: "You are not one of us. We have our own language. Until you can decipher what we're saying, and speak it fluently yourself, you'll remain on the outside. To be part of the club, you must know and speak the secret lingo."

To which many unchurched, non-Christian, marginally Christian or newly-saved Christian people say "Why bother?" And we've lost them.

Language is a powerful tool. Watch yours.

Conclusion

5

Well, there you have it. An average of about four lessons per year over the past decade. Let's see, that's roughly one lesson per quarter. Yeah, I figure that's about right for me. Hate to get on the educational fast track, you know...

Remember what I wrote in the Preface, that once you saw this list you'd probably say to yourself "I can do better than that"? Now you have tangible proof that you can. And I hope you do.

When I was in high school, one of my heroes was a jazz guitarist named Larry Coryell. On weekends, I used to take the bus into New York City, walk about 40 blocks down to the clubs where he played in Greenwich Village, stand in line for several hours to ensure a good seat, and watch him play for a couple of hours, absolutely dazzled by his technique and his lyrical inventiveness. As an aspiring musician (or so I thought), that was as close to heaven as I figured I'd ever get.

I knew I would never be able to play the guitar in the same universe (quality-wise), but I had immense respect for his determination to grow in new areas of his craft. Once, when he was explaining what made him continue to push himself as a musician, he uttered something that was pretty much common sense. At the time, though, it seemed profound to me. Anyway, whether it was or was not is not the point. The point is that his statement stuck with me through the years.

"I always consider myself a student. Once you believe you have mastered something, you have lost your edge and have begun to deteriorate."

I pray that you will always consider yourself to be a student—of life, of people, of the Bible, of yourself, of our culture, of Jesus, of your profession. And perhaps as you consider what you have learned over the last decade, you, too, will recognize that the journey is more important than the destination.